SCAT SINGING FOR KIDS

A STEP-BY-STEP JOURNEY IN JAZZ
BY SHARON BURCH

FREDDIE THE FROG AND THE FLYING JAZZ KITTEN

by Sharon Burch
illustrated by Tiffany Harris
with special guest, Sherry Luchette's Flying Jazz Kitten

• 5TH ADVENTURE: SCAT CAT ISLAND •

TEACHER'S GUIDE

With Storybook Illustrations by Tiffany Harris

No part of this publication may be reproduced in any form or by any means without the prior written permission of the Publisher.

Copyright © 2012 by HAL LEONARD CORPORATION
International Copyright Secured   All Rights Reserved

Shawnee Press

EXCLUSIVELY DISTRIBUTED BY

7777 W. BLUEMOUND RD. P.O. BOX 13819 MILWAUKEE, WI 53213

Visit Hal Leonard Online at
www.halleonard.com

Visit Shawnee Press Online at
www.shawneepress.com

TABLE OF CONTENTS

4 INTRODUCTION
Why teach jazz to kids?
Jazz education sequence
Materials needed
The Mirror Game

8 STEP 1: INTRODUCE FREDDIE THE FROG®
Freddie the Frog® and the Thump in the Night
Freddie the Frog® Teacher's Puppet

10 STEP 2: 4/4 BEAT
Freddie the Frog® and the Mysterious Wahooooo
Beat activities

11 STEP 3: STRESS ON BEATS 2 & 4
Freddie the Frog® and the Secret of Crater Island
"The Gecko Blues" – beats 2 & 4
Suggested recordings with stress on beats 2 & 4

13 STEP 4: SWING FEEL "BEAR, PAPA BEAR, PAPA"
Rhythm Instruments: Chant and Play Swing
Classroom Instrument Rotation
Suggested swing recordings

15 STEP 5: INTRODUCING SCAT THROUGH A STORY
Preparing for the story
Freddie the Frog® and the Flying Jazz Kitten
Instrument scat

18 STEP 6: ECHO SCAT — LEADER/GROUP
 Teacher leader/Group echo
 Student leader/Group echo

21 STEP 7: ECHO SCAT — PARTNERS
 Choosing partners — Scat word flashcards
 Freddie leader/Kitten echo
 Kitten leader/Freddie echo
 New partners

23 STEP 8: ECHO SCAT — NEW SCAT WORDS
 Freddie leader/Kitten echo
 Kitten leader/Freddie echo
 New partners

25 STEP 9: CALL AND RESPONSE — PARTNERS
 Freddie call/Kitten response
 Kitten call/Freddie response
 New partners
 Switch and choose

27 STEP 10: ECHO SCAT — STUDENT LEADERS/GROUP
 Many student leaders/group echo

29 STEP 11: ADDING CLASSROOM INSTRUMENTS
 One leader/group echo with instruments
 Partners — Echo with instruments
 Partners — Call and Response with instruments

31 ADDITIONAL JAZZ RESOURCES FOR KIDS

32 FREDDIE RESOURCES

WHY TEACH JAZZ TO KIDS?

The great jazz artist, Charles Mingus, said it well:

"Making the simple complicated is commonplace; Making the complicated simple, awesomely simple, that's creativity."

Charles Mingus, 1922–1979

Natural, creative play is endangered in a technological age. Music, dance and the arts were once part of children's daily lives. It is up to us to intentionally stimulate the creative development to prepare our next generation's innovative leaders. Jazz music hones these skills better than any other form of music. Scatting and playing jazz develops:

- Creativity
- Synergy
- Musicianship
- Teamwork
- Theory in action
- Fun!

WHY USE FREDDIE?

Freddie makes jazz fun for kids. Kids fall in love with music because they have fallen in love with Freddie the Frog.® They fall in love with jazz through this swingin' adventure. Freddie the Frog® and his Flying Jazz Kitten story introduces kids to jazz through scat. This book contains detailed steps that lead the most insecure student to uninhibited scat singing fun!

Enjoy!
Sharon Burch
Elementary Music Teacher and
Creator/Author of Freddie the Frog® Books

ABOUT SHARON BURCH

Sharon Burch began teaching general music in 1987. Constantly pursuing the best methods of educationally connecting with students, she is a National Board Certified Teacher in Early and Middle Childhood Music, a certified teacher with the International Piano Teaching Foundation, holds a master's degree as a Professional Educator and uses a combination of strategies to enable kids to experience concepts in the classroom. Sharon introduced **Freddie the Frog®** to her classroom of music students and discovered the magic of games, storytelling and puppetry in teaching. She authored *Freddie the Frog and the Thump in the Night*, *Freddie the Frog and the Bass Clef Monster*, *Freddie the Frog and the Mysterious Wahooooo*, and *Freddie the Frog and the Secret of Crater Island* as the first of several adventuresome stories introducing fundamental music concepts. *Freddie the Frog and the Flying Jazz Kitten* introduces jazz through scat and improvisation. Sharon serves on the national Jazz Education Network Elementary Jazz Committee and enjoys sharing her teaching strategies at music conferences and clinics with teachers around the globe.

JAZZ EDUCATION SEQUENCE

This is a basic guideline of a typical jazz education sequence. There are variations based on what the students know and their prior experiences, but it is a good guideline to follow to get started.

1. 4/4 beat
2. Stress on beats 2 & 4
3. Swing feel "Bear, Papa Bear, Papa ..."
4. Echo Response
5. Triplet Undertones "doodle-dah" to "doo—dah"
6. Call and Response Answers
7. Improvisation

These steps make teaching scat singing simple and fun.

FREDDIE THE FROG®
Books and Materials referred to in this book:

→ *Freddie the Frog®* Teacher's Puppet
→ *Freddie the Frog® and the Flying Jazz Kitten* book/audio CD
→ Scat Words Flashcard Set
→ *Freddie the Frog® and the Thump in the Night* book/audio CD
→ *Freddie the Frog® and the Mysterious Wahooooo* book/audio CD
→ *Freddie the Frog® and the Secret of Crater Island* book/audio CD

For more product information, see pages 31–32.

Games and Coloring Pages
www.FreddieTheFrog.com

Video clips, Audio clips and other teaching tools
www.TeachingWithFreddieTheFrog.com

BUT, BEFORE WE DIG INTO THE WORLD OF JAZZ ...

Freddie the Frog® makes teaching jazz to kids simple. Before you dig into jazz and the scat lessons, it's essential that the kids connect to Freddie first.

→ **Skip step 1** if your students already know Freddie and his first story.
→ **Skip steps 1, 2 and 3** if your students have already experienced the Freddie books and the extension lessons listed in steps 2 and 3.
→ **Play "The Mirror Game"** to establish silent communication and classroom management when incorporating actions. It works like magic!

CLASSROOM MANAGEMENT MAGIC — THE MIRROR GAME

Kids love "the mirror game," and once established, it is an incredibly efficient use of time. It prepares your kids for silent instruction used throughout the teacher's guide.

RULES OF THE MIRROR GAME

1. Teacher is the "leader" and students are the teacher's giant mirror.

2. Rules to establish before beginning.
   Ask the students the following questions:
   A. **"Do mirrors talk?"** *(No)*
   B. **"Do mirrors echo?"** *(No)*
   C. Say, **"The better you are, the more I will try to trick you."**

3. Begin by putting both hands up and in front of your body as a starting signal. Hold your position until everyone is doing the same.

4. Start with both hands and arms doing the same thing, such as leaning to the right slowly, with your hands still in front of you.

5. As they catch on and are silently being a mirror, switch to one arm or hand doing something different than the other, make silly faces, etc. Increase the difficulty to make it fun. Pull your hands apart like you are going to clap, and then pass the hands by each other without clapping. A few kids typically predict a clap and giggles abound.

6. Announce "Game Over."

7. Explain that throughout the story, or sometimes in the middle of the song, you will suddenly play the "mirror game."

This works like a dream when preparing for performances. Teach the actions, but also let them know that you are playing the mirror game during a performance so that all actions are synchronized.

STEP 1:
INTRODUCE FREDDIE THE FROG®

↠ **Freddie the Frog® and the Thump in the Night**

↠ **Teaching with the Freddie the Frog® Teacher's Puppet**

Although the book/CD, *Freddie the Frog® and the Flying Jazz Kitten*, can be used independently, it will be more "magical" for the kids if you pull them into Freddie's world through the first book, *Freddie the Frog and the Thump in the Night*, prior to the jazz story. The first story introduces the kids to Freddie, his best friend, Eli the Elephant, their personalities and where they live. The story gives the puppet a personality and he becomes "real."

Freddie becomes the kids' friend and they eagerly come to music to see Freddie. They come to see Freddie and find out what fun things he wants to do in music that day.

Share the story *Freddie the Frog® and the Thump in the Night* with your students.

The teacher's book, *Beyond the Books*, spells out 14 sequential lessons based on the first four stories in the Freddie the Frog® series. It is a worthwhile investment in extending the learning far beyond the storybooks. It also includes a CD-ROM with teacher downloads for review and assessment. It makes teaching music fun for you and the kids!

 **FREDDIE NOTE**

In case you just started using Freddie, here's an important tip:

Pretend that only you, the teacher, can "hear" Freddie's voice. The kids hear his voice on the audio CD. Using your voice for Freddie will make him less magical, or "real," in the kids' minds, because your voice for Freddie will not match Freddie's voice on the audio CD.

There are three good reasons to use Freddie this way:

1. Freddie's voice remains consistent with the voice on the CD, so he seems more real. The "real" factor makes it magical for the kids
2. Easier for the teacher.
3. If a substitute is teaching or a student moves to another school where the music teacher is using Freddie, then there is still consistency with the "voice" of Freddie, because it is only imagined and used the same way by each teacher.

See Sharon demonstrate and explain using Freddie on the video link, "Music Teachers Meet Freddie the Frog" at **www.K3MusicTeachers.com**.

STEP 2: 4/4 BEAT

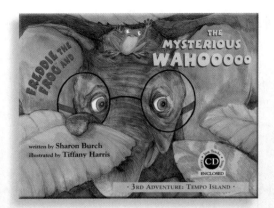

→ *Freddie the Frog® and the Mysterious Wahooooo*

→ Beat activities

For the purposes of preparing the students for jazz, or any music experience, it is important that the students are very comfortable finding and keeping the beat. *Freddie the Frog® and the Mysterious Wahooooo* book/audio CD gets kids involved in recognizing simple rhythm patterns, different tempo terms and feeling the beat. It is also perfect for correlating the terminology with a beat experience.

Kids love this book because it's fun, interactive and they get to play rhythm instruments. Teachers love this book because kids experience the difference between beat and rhythm, performing them simultaneously! At the end of the story, the students clearly understand the difference simply by connecting to which character represented beat, which is Eli the Elephant, and which character represented the rhythm, which is Freddie the Frog.

Before beginning the story, divide the class into two sections. One section plays the beat with Eli using rhythms sticks or chopsticks or unsharpened pencils. The other half of the class uses small shakers, such as mini-maracas or little egg shakers. Explain to the students that when Eli starts to play the beat, they play the beat with him. The students with the shakers play with Freddie when he plays the rhythm. When they hear the word, "fine," stop. Practice using the instruments described. Instruct the "beat" kids to quietly say "ta" as they play along.

Once the story is finished, use the audio CD tracks "Largo," "Andante," "Allegro" and "Presto" to practice hearing and performing the beat.

(Detailed extension lessons are described in **Beyond the Books** Teacher's Guide.)

Continue to look for opportunities in all styles of music for kids to hear, feel and perform the beat while listening.

STEP 3:
STRESS ON BEATS 2 & 4

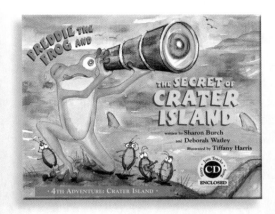

➜ *Freddie the Frog® and the Secret of Crater Island*

➜ *"The Gecko Blues"* audio track. Free download at **freddiethefrog.com/downloads.php**

➜ Suggested recordings with stress on beats 2 & 4

Blues music stresses beats two and four. Introduce the blues style music through the kid-friendly Blue Beetle Bugs song in the *Secret of Crater Island* book/audio CD.

TEACHER NOTE: One of the blue beetle bugs misbehaved and used the words, "shut up," in the Gecko Blues song, audio track #5. It mistakenly made it onto the master CD inside the Freddie the Frog and the Secret of Crater Island storybook.

> Use the free "cleaned up" Gecko Blues download at
> www.FreddieTheFrog.com/downloads.php

Give a brief explanation of the origination of the blues in American history, and how it shares something that made the musician feel sad or "blue." The Blue Beetle Bugs were blue about the Geckos keeping them from following the Damselflies to Crater Island.

To help students feel beats two and four, ask them to "mirror" the following actions while listening to their song:

1. Tap the beat with two fingers of one hand on one thigh.
   (For example, two fingers on the right hand are tapping the right thigh.)
   Once you see that all students are successfully keeping the beat, move to Step 2.

2. Raise the two fingers in the air and across the body on beats one and three, and only tap the thigh on beats two and four. (For example, two fingers of the right hand lift and cross in the air above the left thigh on beats one and three; then taps the right thigh on beats two and four.) This is a great way to feel the stress on two and four. It is also an excellent opportunity to silently help guide a student's hand during the song.

(Detailed instructions on how to guide the students in writing their own blues song located in the **Beyond the Book** Teacher's Guide.)

Now that the students are introduced to the sound and feel of the stress on beats two and four, find other recordings to "discover" the same jazzy feel. There are many to choose from.

Here is a short list of recordings to get you started:

→ "One Shoe Blues" Sandra Boynton/B.B. King (Check out the video!)

→ Album collection: *Jazz and Swing for Kids* by Genius + Love
  - "Diddle, Diddle, Swing"
  - "Here Comes the Rain Itsy"
  - "Old MacDonald Jazz Remix"
  - "Rockin' Robin"
  - "Twinkle, Twinkle, Swingin' Star"

Kids love all of the songs listed, and they all stress beats two and four.

STEP 4:
SWING FEEL –
"BEAR, PAPA BEAR, PAPA"

- Rhythm Instruments: Chant and Play Swing
- Classroom Instrument Rotation
- Suggested swing recordings

Swing is an important jazz element. In jazz, if there are two eighth notes together, they are typically "swung," meaning that the first eighth note is slightly longer than the second.

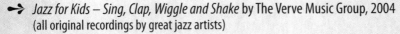

Hearing and "feeling" the swing is the best way to learn how to "swing." Play swing music recordings and have students move and chant to the swing to help them hear and feel swing.

Here are a few suggested swing recordings that work well with kids:

- *Swing for Kids* by the Swiss Army Big Band
  - "Pink Panther"
  - "Fly Me to the Moon"
  - "Peter Gunn"

- *Jazz for Kids – Sing, Clap, Wiggle and Shake* by The Verve Music Group, 2004 (all original recordings by great jazz artists)
  - "The Muffin Man" (ELLA FITZGERALD)
  - "Ain't Nobody Here But Us Chickens" (LOUIS JORDAN & HIS TYMPANY FIVE)
  - "Potato Chips" (SLIM GAILLARD)
  - "What a Wonderful World" (LOUIS ARMSTRONG)

Listen and move to swing music.
1. Play the selected swing recording.
2. TAP the beat with two fingers.
3. Only tap or snap beats two and four as indicated in Step 3 (page 11).

4. **CHANT,** "Bear, **Pa**pa Bear, **Pa**pa Bear . . ." along with the music. Remember, the stress is on the first "Pa" of "Papa."
(Audio example at: **www.TeachingWithFreddieTheFrog.com**)

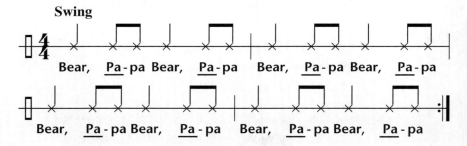

5. Give each student a classroom rhythm instrument.
6. Play and chant "Bear, Papa Bear, Papa Bear . . ."
7. Say "pass," after every four or eight bars. Students pass their instrument to the student on the left. (This keeps the instrument playing interesting for the kids as they get to play a variety of instruments.)
8. THINK the chant as you play your instrument along with the recording.

 *Make sure that the students understand the direction of the rotation by practicing it without the music playing first.*

WHY ROTATE CLASSROOM INSTRUMENTS?

→ Kids are excited to play classroom rhythm instruments and they each have their favorites. By establishing a rotation pattern that is used consistently, it saves time and avoids students fighting over who gets to play what.

→ It also creates a natural repetition as each child gets a turn to play a different type of instrument. The students are excited to play different instruments. The real benefit is that the students get better with repetition, especially engaged repetition. The rotation of the instruments keeps the repetition exciting for the kids.

→ Seat the children in a circle and pass out the instruments to every other or every third student. They pat or tap when they don't have an instrument. When you say "pass," they always pass to the left.

STEP 5:
INTRODUCING SCAT THROUGH A STORY

→ Preparing for the story

→ *Freddie the Frog® and the Flying Jazz Kitten*

→ Instrument scat

PREPARING FOR THE STORY

Freddie wants to share a story about the day he met a flying jazz kitten.

If sharing the story with preschool or kindergarten, just enjoy the story with the audio track. Before the story begins, briefly explain that during the story we get to pretend to play different instruments with our voices.

Demonstrate and practice being the instruments before the story begins:

- → **Drummer:** Two fingers pretend to be drum sticks in the air keeping the beat and vocalizing the hi-hat chanting, "shh, shh, shh…" in a swing rhythm matching the audio.
- → **Bass player:** Mimic playing the upright bass with two hands and singing, "a-boom, boom, boom, boom…" in a walking bass pattern that matches the audio.
- → **Pianist:** Mimic playing with two hands on the keyboard and singing, "skiddley, skiddley, plunk…" matching the audio.
- → **Trumpet:** Mimic playing with three fingers of the right hand (teacher mirrors it to the students with your left hand) and scat singing, "zwee-bop, zwee-bop…" matching the audio.
- → **Trombone:** Everyone picks up their imaginary trombone and echoes, "wah-wah," and then listens to the next part of the story.

Now, ages 8 and up are ready to be divided into four scat singing groups:

1. Drum set hi hat part
2. Bass
3. Piano
4. Trumpet

Everyone echoes the trombone "Wah, Wah," signaling that it is time to listen to the next part of the story.

Practice the layering of the instrumental scat singing before beginning the story. Use your fingers holding up one finger, two fingers, three fingers or four fingers to silently indicate when each group begins. Demonstrate and practice a "cut-off" to insure that the students understand when to start and when to end. Use the same cues during the story.

Begin the story. Just let the kids listen and enjoy the story the first time until they get to the jazz club. Then cue each group to join in with their part. Remember, younger kids all switch instruments; older kids layer the parts.

Demonstrate the actions of the city sounds the first time. The second time the city sounds happen, indicate for the students to echo and do the actions with you (mirror game).

City sound actions that I use:

- ***Beep, beep, honk, honk:*** Right hand palm pushes an imaginary horn in front, off to the right, two times; Left hand does the same two times, but to the left.
- ***Blink, blink:*** Right hand "blinks" by opening a fist into an open, spread palm; Left hand does the same.
- ***Ding, ding, clang, clang:*** Right hand pretends to hold an imaginary school bell in the air while the left hand holds the right elbow at a 90 degree angle. Right hand swings side to side two times to match the chant.
- ***Zip, zap:*** Both hands grasp each other while bending elbows at about a 90-degree angle and the grasped hands switch from one side to the other for "zip, zap."
- ***Tweet, tweet, yeow:*** Pat thighs twice with both hands on "tweet, tweet" then palms up in the air in front of you on "yeow."

Check out the 2-minute video clip at www.TeachingWithFreddieTheFrog.com to see the actions demonstrated. Feel free to make up your own actions that match the chant.

While students are listening to the scatting at the end of the story, invite the entire group to join in with each part as a unison group.

1. Drums
2. Bass
3. Piano
4. Trumpet
5. Decrescendo until the trombone part, in which everyone echoes the trombone.

The third trombone echo part is vocalized after the last "wah-wah."

Now the ice is broken, the kids (of any age) have been introduced to scat singing. It's time to lead them to independent, uninhibited scattin' fun!

NO SKIPPING STEPS!

Implement every step outlined in STEPS 6-11 no matter what the age!

The younger the student, the more uninhibited they will be. Students eight and under will echo whatever you sing with no reservation. The older the student, the more you will need to lead them step-by-step to raise their comfort level in scat singing.

You may spend less time on certain steps with various groups, but no skipping. Read the comfort level of everyone in the room. Move to the next step when you feel all have reached a high comfort level and are ready to move on. When you sense that some are bored, switch partners. This will help insecure scat singers feel more comfortable with a more secure new partner.

STEP 6:
ECHO SCAT — LEADER / GROUP

↪ Teacher leader/group echo
↪ Student leader/group echo

The story naturally led the students into scat singing along with Freddie and the jazz cats. Now the fun begins!

TEACHER NOTE: *If scat singing is new to you, listen to the audio track #3, "Echo Scat," on the* **Freddie the Frog and the Flying Jazz Kitten** *book's audio CD, and practice echoing Freddie. Notice that each phrase is about one measure, or one bar, long. The shorter the phrase, the easier it is to echo. When comfortable leading scat singing phrases as Freddie did on the recording, ask the student group to echo.*

TEACHER LEADER / GROUP ECHO
(Include hand/body motions)

Display the following scat word set at the front of the room.

DOOBY	BIP	WAP	SCOO	SHOOBY
WOOBY	BOP	WOP	DIDDLEY	SKIDDLEY
SCOOBY	BUM	BAM	DO-DAT	WAH-WAH

1. Play **"Blues Track in C"** (*Freddie the Frog® and the Flying Jazz Kitten* book's audio CD)
2. Model and ask the students to feel the beat in their shoulders.
3. Model and ask the students to snap or tap on beats two and four.
4. Starting with "DOOBY," scat sing and wait for students to echo. Keep your phrases to four counts, keeping it easy for students to echo, similar to Freddie on track #3.
5. Proceed left to right with the next scat word "BIP."
6. Add hand/arm/body actions that reflect the melodic direction of your scat phrase; indicate for students to echo and mimic actions.
7. Continue until you have made it all the way through the list, working left to right.
8. Go back and choose random words from the list, or create new words.
9. When you see that at least one student is uninhibited and enjoying the scat singing, invite the student to lead instead of you.

WHY ARE THESE STEPS IMPORTANT?

→ It is very important that students establish and feel the beat first. Establishing the stress on beats two and four, establishes the swing feel of jazz.

→ If your students can read, giving them an order that they can visually anticipate the next scat word gives the students more security about singing non-sense syllables.

→ **Physical actions raise the comfort level and reinforce pitch direction.**

→ Going "in order" gives the students a little confidence. By still using the list but mixing it up, you are taking the students one small step forward.

→ Continue leading until you see at least one student who is uninhibited and enjoying the scat singing.

STUDENT LEADER / GROUP ECHO

(Include hand/body motions)

Display the following scat word set at the front of the room.

DOOBY	BIP	WAP	SCOO	SHOOBY
WOOBY	BOP	WOP	DIDDLEY	SKIDDLEY
SCOOBY	BUM	BAM	DO-DAT	WAH-WAH

1. Invite the chosen "uninhibited" student to come to the front and take your place.
2. Tell the new leader he/she has a choice, and may do either of the following:
   A. Use a word from the list on the board or from the story.
   B. Make up their own scat word, but it can't be a "real" word.
3. Ask the leader to use hand/arm/body actions to reflect the melodic direction of the scat phrase; and indicate for students to echo and mimic actions.
4. Start the **"Blues Track in C"** and count off when the student should begin.
5. Allow the student leader to lead several times and encourage as needed.
6. Clap for the student when he or she finishes. (This sets a standard for clapping for the soloist while encouraging the student.)

WHY A STUDENT LEADER?

→ Choosing a student leader gives a student the chance to shine in front of the others. Often, it is the typical "class clown" or attention-loving student that is most uninhibited and loves the chance to be in the front. This is a great opportunity for that student and everyone involved.

→ This also hints at the goal for everyone in the room.

→ Do NOT criticize the student's leading. Just go with whatever they do (as long as it is appropriate, of course). If they are way off in pitch, or rhythm, etc., just let it happen for now. The next steps will guide them to where they need to be.

STEP 7:
ECHO SCAT — PARTNERS

- Choosing partners – Scat word flashcards
- Freddie leader/Kitten echo
- Kitten leader/Freddie echo
- New partners

TEACHER NOTE: *If beginning step 7 on a new day, review and repeat step 6 before starting step 7. Establish that the students' comfort level is high in the group echo before pairing students. Reviewing the group echo scat lesson will prepare the students for this step.*

Display the following scat word set at the front of the room.

DOOBY	BIP	WAP	SCOO	SHOOBY
WOOBY	BOP	WOP	DIDDLEY	SKIDDLEY
SCOOBY	BUM	BAM	DO-DAT	WAH-WAH

CHOOSING PARTNERS — SCAT WORD FLASHCARDS

1. Distribute an equal number of Freddie and Kitten flashcards, one card per student.
2. Ask them to read their scat word on the back of the card. Take turns saying it aloud. Help as needed.
3. Students hold their card in front of them with the Kitten or Freddie showing.
4. Have each "Freddie" find a "Kitten" and stand facing each other.

FREDDIE LEADER / KITTEN ECHO

5. Freddie/Kitten partners lay their cards on the floor by their feet, careful not to step on them.
6. Instruct the Freddies to lead, once the music starts, using the word "Shooby." Add an action with their hands and arms to go with their scat word. The action should match the melodic direction. (e.g., voice up, hands up; voice down, hands, down) Kittens echo and mimic actions of their Freddie partner.
7. Play **"Blues Track in C"** and **count off when to begin**. Ask the Freddies to lead with the word "Shooby." Kittens echo.

KITTEN LEADER / FREDDIE ECHO

8. After 12 bars, or measures, of music, SAY, "Switch!"
9. Kittens do the same thing, leading with the same word or a new word that you give to them for 12 bars.

SWITCH WHO LEADS EVERY 12 BARS

10. Switch leader every 12 bars, Freddie or Kitten, until the students feel fairly comfortable.
11. Give them a new scat word each time they switch.

NEW PARTNERS

12. Pick up their cards and have each Freddie find a new Kitten and vice versa. Hold their card in front of them so others can see if they are a kitten or frog.

WHY SWITCH PARTNERS?

→ Each time the students switch partners, there is peer coaching, modeling and a social interaction that changes the dynamics in the room. Using the cards to find new partners helps to eliminate the social politics.

→ Confident scat singers encourage not-so-confident scat singers and give them courage to stretch out of their comfort zone. Typically, everyone wants to scat and move, but some feel self-conscious. The switching of partners and following the steps outlined helps everyone in the room stretch their comfort zone and have fun.

→ Choosing partners tends to create a classroom management problem and wastes time. Using the Freddie and Kitten cards help to solve both of those problems.

STEP 8:
ECHO SCAT — NEW SCAT WORDS

→ Freddie leader/Kitten echo
→ Kitten leader/Freddie echo
→ New partners

MULTIPLE COMFORT LEVELS

It's important to give the students a choice. At this point, you will have a variety of comfort levels. By giving them a choice of what scat words to use, they are free to continue to lean on the word "crutches" provided or free to move to the next level. You will probably notice that some students were already glancing at the word list at the front of the room and using different words before Step 8. That's great! That's why they were posted. Let it naturally happen. They use new words when they are ready to move on.

Display the following scat word set at the front of the room.

DOOBY	BIP	WAP	SCOO	SHOOBY
WOOBY	BOP	WOP	DIDDLEY	SKIDDLEY
SCOOBY	BUM	BAM	DO-DAT	WAH-WAH

FREDDIE LEADER / KITTEN ECHO
(Include hand/body motions)

1. Each student has a new partner.
2. Read their scat word to each other. Help each other if needed.
3. Instruct students to lay their cards by their feet.
4. Freddies lead first and may choose any of the following:
   A. Use the scat word on their flashcard.
   B. Use a word from the list on the board or from the story.
   C. Make up their own scat word, but it can't be a "real" word.
5. Freddies lead with their chosen word or words, creating actions to go with their scat word.
6. Kittens echo and copy the actions.
7. Play **"Blues Track in C"** and count off when the Freddies should begin.
8. Say **"Switch!"** after 12 bars.

KITTEN LEADER / FREDDIE ECHO
(Include hand/body motions)

1. Continue playing "Blues Track in C."
2. Kittens lead as the Freddies did, each leading with a scat word of their choice and creating actions that reflect the melodic direction.

SWITCH WHO LEADS EVERY 12 BARS

1. Direct switching back and forth between Freddie and Kitten, taking turns leading with their word and actions every 12 bars.
2. Make sure the Freddies and Kittens get equal turns leading.

    Remember, to count off the first person to lead. It will help them get started with confidence and on the right beat.

NEW PARTNERS

1. Pick up their card and each Freddie finds a new Kitten and vice versa. Hold their card in front of them so others can see if they are a kitten or frog.
2. Repeat step 8 with new partners.

READ THE COMFORT LEVEL

READ your room and let the comfort level of your group, regardless of age, determine when to repeat or move to the next step.

WHY FLASHCARDS?

→ The flashcard serves as a "crutch" or "security blanket." They have a word that their teacher "told them to use."

→ The flashcards only serve as a starting point, as you will find out as you progress through the steps.

→ It's amazing how the physical cards and physical actions bring security when feeling like you are out of your comfort zone.

STEP 9:
CALL AND RESPONSE — PARTNERS

→ Freddie call/Kitten response   → New partners
→ Kitten call/Freddie response   → Switch and choose

INTRODUCTION TO CALL AND RESPONSE

Now that students are comfortable using a variety of scat words, it is easy to progress to call and response. Use the words on the flashcards to get started. Switching of partners and using actions will also help at this level.

Remind students to use their hands/arms/body along with their scat word.

> **Display the following scat word set at the front of the room.**
>
> | | | | | |
> |---|---|---|---|---|
> | DOOBY | BIP | WAP | SCOO | SHOOBY |
> | WOOBY | BOP | WOP | DIDDLEY | SKIDDLEY |
> | SCOOBY | BUM | BAM | DO-DAT | WAH-WAH |

FREDDIE CALL / KITTEN RESPONSE
(Include hand/body motions)

1. Freddie leads with the scat word on his or her card.
2. Kitten answers with the scat word on his or her card.
3. This time the hand/arm/body actions will only go with that person's word. Still use actions even though they are no longer copying each other.
4. Play **"Blues Track in C"** and count off to begin.

KITTEN CALL / FREDDIE RESPONSE
(Include hand/body motions)

1. Kitten leads with the scat word on his or her card.
2. Freddie answers with the scat word on his or her card.
3. Hand/arm/body actions will only go with that person's word. Continue using actions though they are no longer copying each other.
4. Play **"Blues Track in C"** and count off to begin.

NEW PARTNERS

Pick up their cards and each Freddie finds a new Kitten and vice versa. Hold their card in front of them so others can see if they are a kitten or frog.

SWITCH AND CHOOSE

1. Continue to play "Blues Track in C."
2. Create actions and choose any scat word that they want in a call and response:
   A. Use the scat word on their card.
   B. Use a word from the list on the board or from the story.
   C. Make up a new scat word, but it can't be a "real" word.
3. Say "Switch" after every 12 bars.
4. Watching the comfort level of the room, say **"Find a new partner,"** after every set of 24 bars.
5. When you can see that everyone is comfortable scatting and adding actions, it is time for step 10!

CREATIVE ACTION IDEAS

→ Mix it up and give them specific body parts to move, such as only their elbows.

→ It adds an extra element of fun and brain-stretching creativity to structure what body parts students can use to create actions.

→ Ideas:
  - Only use knees.
  - Only lower half of your body.
  - Only fingers.
  - Only legs.
  - Be creative!

STEP 10:
ECHO SCAT – STUDENT LEADERS / GROUP ECHO

This is the best part! Magic happens in the room at this point. **ONLY do this step if the students have a high comfort level in the previous steps.**

If beginning this step on a new day, review and repeat steps 8 & 9 to assess students' comfort levels and readiness. Once you observe the students easily scatting with their partners and having fun, that's the cue to do this step.

Again, display the following scat word set at the front of the room. Ask students to suggest additions to the list.

DOOBY	BIP	WAP	SCOO	SHOOBY
WOOBY	BOP	WOP	DIDDLEY	SKIDDLEY
SCOOBY	BUM	BAM	DO-DAT	WAH-WAH

1. Ask all students to face you at the front of the room.
2. Play **"Blues Track in C."**
3. Lead group echo as you did in step 6.
4. Invite students, one at a time, to come to the front and take your place. Remind the student leaders that they may choose from the following:
   - A. Use a word from the list on the board or from the story.
   - B. Make up a new scat word, but it can't be a "real" word.

→ *Try to give everyone a short turn at the front.*

➻ **Always CLAP after each soloist while the music continues to play.**
It not only encourages and acknowledges the soloist, but also establishes the jazz audience standard etiquette of clapping immediately after a soloist plays their improvised solo in a performance.

A MAGICAL TRANSFORMATION

As the music teacher, you have the privilege to facilitate an amazing transformation by the end of these steps. Speaking in front of a group of people is the number one fear of many. Asking people of any age above eight to sing non-sense syllables, as a soloist in front of a group of people, is incredibly unnerving for most.

The process of leading the group from outside their comfort zone to uninhibited fun with their singing voice creates a unique bond and synergy amidst the group. You created a "safe zone" to help others try something new in an area that most people fear. They faced their fears together and conquered, and they had fun.

They will leave your room scatting!

STEP 11:
ADDING CLASSROOM INSTRUMENTS

- One leader/group echo with instruments
- Partners – Echo with instruments
- Partners – Call and Response with instruments

On another day, another lesson ...

Add small rhythm instruments and go through the steps again but with instruments. It adds a whole new level, teaching the kids to THINK and HEAR the melodic line internally while playing an instrument. This is wonderful preparation for instrumental playing.

Here's a quick outline of sequential steps when adding classroom instruments:

ONE LEADER / GROUP ECHO WITH INSTRUMENTS

1. **Teacher leader scats/plays rhythm instrument;** student group scats and plays echo responses with rhythm instruments.

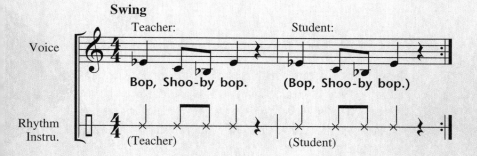

2. Rotate rhythm instruments to the left after every few bars. (See page 14.)
3. **Student leader scats/plays rhythm instrument;** group scats and plays echo responses.
4. Rotate rhythm instruments to the left after every few bars.
5. Repeat steps 1-4, but this time **only THINK the scat words** while playing the instrument.

PARTNERS ECHO WITH INSTRUMENTS

1. Divide into partners using flashcards or a numbering system. (See Teacher's Management Note below.)
2. Partners assume leader/echo roles with instruments. Scat and play rhythm instruments.
3. Switch roles.
4. New partners.
5. Partners **THINK the scat words** and play rhythm instrument echoes.
6. Switch roles.

PARTNERS CALL AND RESPONSE WITH INSTRUMENTS

1. Partners **scat and play** call and response with the instruments.
2. Switch roles
3. Partners **THINK the scat words** while playing call and response.
4. Switch roles
5. New partners

TEACHER MANAGEMENT NOTE

→ **Remember to rotate partners and instruments.** Students will be distracted while wondering if they get to play a certain favorite instrument or not. If they understand the system of rotation and realize that everyone gets to play every instrument, they will focus on playing the instrument in their hand.

→ **Using displayed words in the front of the room will work better when playing instruments.** Cards and instruments may be too many things to keep organized.

→ **Assign half the group to be "1s" and the other half, "2s." "1s" find a "2" partner.** Partners find each other by holding their number in the air using their fingers.

ADDITIONAL JAZZ RESOURCES FOR KIDS

➜ www.K8Jazz.com
- List of Jazz Storybooks and Books
- Lesson Ideas and website links

YouTube videos of great jazz performances. Search for scat singing artists, **Ella Fitzgerald, Sarah Vaughan and Louis Armstrong,** to begin.

COLORING PAGES AND PARENT NOTES

Downloadable coloring pages for each Freddie the Frog® book available at the **www.FreddieTheFrog.com**. Click on the word COLORING, and then click on the coloring page underneath one of the books. The single coloring page will open up to various coloring pages that go with the chosen book.

FREDDIE THE FROG® TEACHER JAZZ SET
(Adventure 5)
00102436 . . . . $49.99

THE FLYING JAZZ KITTEN
This Freddie adventure introduces kids to jazz through interactive scat.
09971606 Book/CD $23.95

FLASHCARD SET: SCAT WORDS
25 Scat Word full color flashcards and lesson ideas corresponding to Freddie's adventure with the Jazz Kitten.
09971643 Flashcard Set: Scat Words $16.99

SCAT SINGING FOR KIDS
This step-by-step teacher's guide creates a "safe zone" and leads the most insecure student to uninhibited scattin' fun!
35028558 Teacher Guide (Adventure 5) $12.99

GREAT RESOURCES FROM FREDDIE THE FROG®

SEPARATELY AVAILABLE OR IN HANDY SETS!

THE THUMP IN THE NIGHT
Adventure 1 • 6 Treble Clef Notes
09971507 Book/CD $23.95
09971508 Flashcards $6.95

THE BASS CLEF MONSTER
Adventure 2 • 9 Bass Clef Notes
09971501 Book/CD $23.95
09971502 Flashcards $6.95
09971500 Bass Clef Poster $6.95

14" HAND PUPPET
09971509 .... $19.95

THE MYSTERIOUS WAHOOOOO
Adventure 3 • Tempo, Rhythm & Beat
09971503 Book/CD $23.95
09971504 Magnetic Rhythm Board .. $16.95

THE SECRET OF CRATER ISLAND
Adventure 4 • 6 More Treble Clef Notes
09971505 Book/CD $23.95
09971506 Flashcards $6.95
09971510 Treble Clef Poster $6.95

BEYOND THE BOOKS
Teacher Tips, Tool and Assessment for Adventures 1 – 4
35027959 Teacher Resource/
          CD-ROM $24.99

HANDY SETS available for extra "Freddie" value!

FREDDIE THE FROG® TEACHER STARTER SET
(Adventure 1)
00102432 .... $68.99
- Teacher's Puppet
- *The Thump in the Night* (book/CD & flashcards)
- *Beyond the Books*

FREDDIE THE FROG® TEACHER SET
(Adventures 1-4)
00102434 .... $168.99
- Teacher's Puppet
- *Beyond the Books*
- *The Thump in the Night* (book/CD & flashcards)
- *The Bass Clef Monster* (book/CD & flashcards)
- *The Mysterious Wahooooo* (book/CD & rhythm board)
- *The Secret of Crater Island* (book/CD & flashcards)